M000079449

Dance of the Love Caterpillars

Dance of the *Love* Caterpillars

DAVID CHARLES BROWER

Copyright © 2021 by David Brower.

All rights reserved. No part of this publication may be reproduced, distributed, or transmitted in any form or by any means, including photocopying, recording, digital scanning, or other electronic or mechanical methods, without the prior written permission of the publisher, except in the case of brief quotations embodied in critical reviews and certain other noncommercial uses permitted by copyright law. For permission requests, write to the publisher, addressed "Attention: Permissions Coordinator," to the address below.

Illustrator: Sheryl VanderPol

ISBN Paperback: # 978-2-9576602-0-9

Printed in the United States of America.

David Brower
Email: db@davidbrower.com
Website: www.davidbrower.com

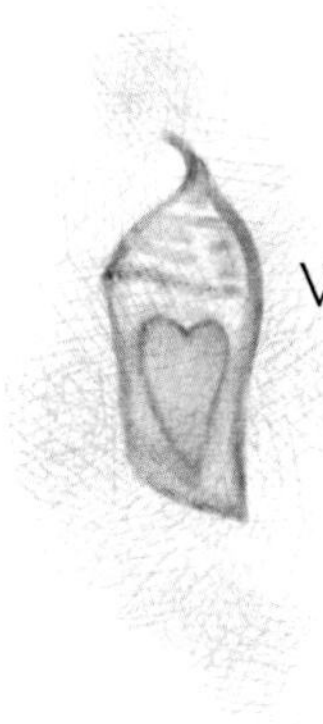

For Her
And for Me
Whatever We are to Be
Always Free
To Love
To Be

My same Wish goes for You
Free to Love
Who You Choose
And to Always,
Forever
Be True
To You

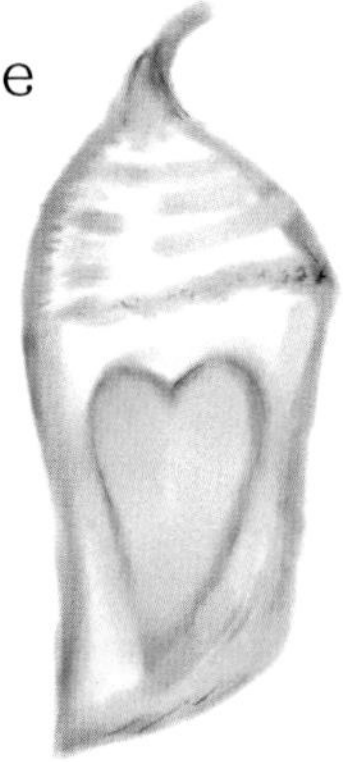

A Note From The Author

The one enduring question that has always been present within me since I can remember is :
"Is there love here?"

Since I was a little boy, my heart has always yearned for the feelings and sensations of being loved.
Of being in love. And loving it!

That feeling of being adored, cherished, held by another. And the meaning and feelings affectionately experienced in loving another so much.

And while much Love was gloriously rained on me throughout my childhood and into my early adulthood, I still often questioned, feared, if I was being loved. And was I loving? Was I going to find "true Love"? And it find me? Would I recognize it? Would it ever be enough?

One day, as Life would have it, my heart was beautifully taken up in a daring, magnificent, life-changing Love that lasted a very long time. Only for illness to steal her from me, forever more.

So it is, Love. And Life.

One has the choice to open one's heart to Love. To start again. And maybe again….
To trust life, again. To believe in Love, again.

And I have. I am.

For me, Love makes life worth living. Even with that vulnerable question vacillating within.

It is the soul elixir that we never seem to get enough of, that manifests in myriad ways.

Love doesn't label. Nor shames. Is not impatient. Nor bullying.

Love nurtures. Forgives. Protects.
Impassions. Jubilates. Supports and
encourages.
Love is playful and full of surprises.
It dares and intoxicates the soul.
Generates abundant energy.
It reassures and calms. Honors and
respects.

It frees you. And brings you to your
senses.

Love is the first and last passage of
our lives, at birth and death. And
permeates everything in between.

My life has been about romantically
finding Love in everything and everyone.
Being Love in my relationships, my
work, my art and creations, all my life's
experiences.

It serves to remind me that Love is
found.

Within me.

Always and forever more.

So while we may, from time to time, lose romantic Love.

Or struggle to embody it in challenging moments.

Love is always, resiliently omnipresent within us, for us.

We are Love - it is neither lost nor found.

It is, simply, us.

We are here to share it with abundant sensorial ***allégresse***.

Savoring the adventure of Love,
David Charles Brower

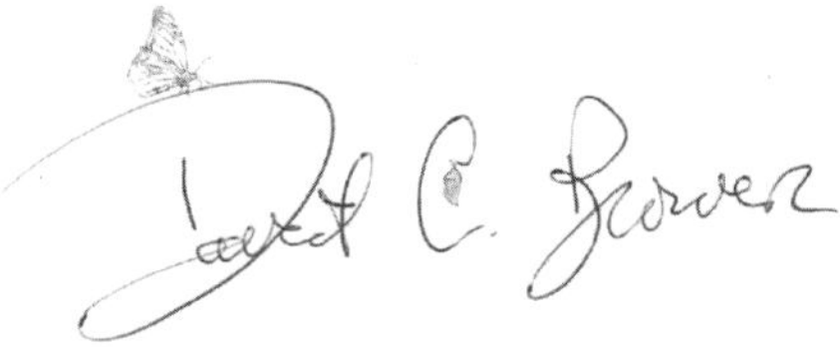

Dance of the *Love* Caterpillars

Two splendid caterpillars crawl
on opposite sides of a river,
for on each of their banks,
the trees have no more leaves,
due to a long dry period.
The caterpillars have climbed
down, exceptionally, in
search of food.

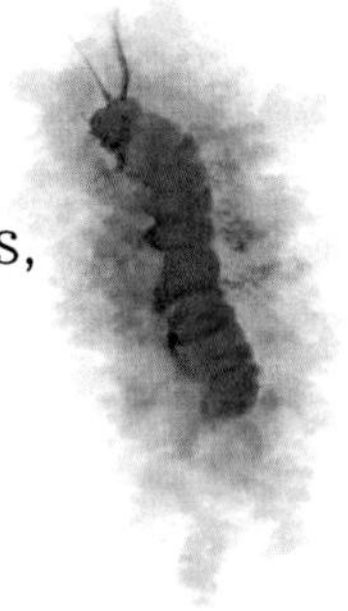

One is crawling up the bank.
The other is crawling down.

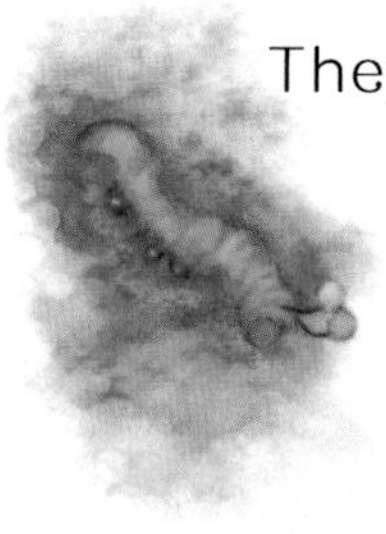

The river is flowing strong.
They hardly notice one another
on the opposite bank
as they cross each other.
One is a magical florescent
blue. The other a vibrant
fuchsia pink.

Caterpillars move in a special way.
When they bend, their guts glide up
first, followed then by their bodies.
They literally follow their guts in life!

It's an unusually hot, humid and sticky day. Lightning suddenly strikes as nature feels the need to put an end to the torrid relentless heat. An enormous lightning bolt hits a Love tree, which falls down across the river.

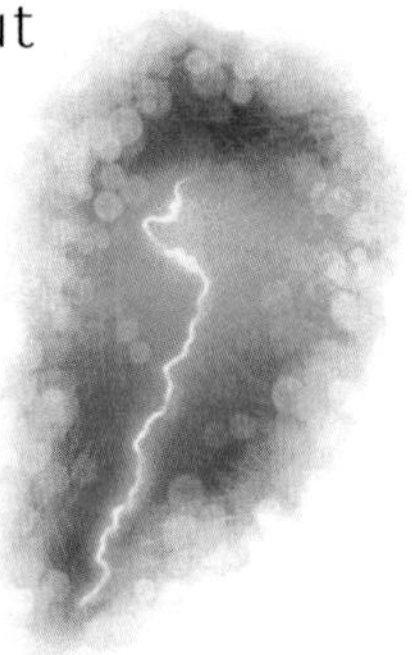

Love trees have purplish-red flowers, their wood valuable for veneers. Veneer is a thin layer of decorative wood. It's a superficial covering, a façade, even a deceptively outward show.

Luckily both survive unscathed, and they realize this Love tree has some tasty colorful flowers left on it, while the leaves are all gone.

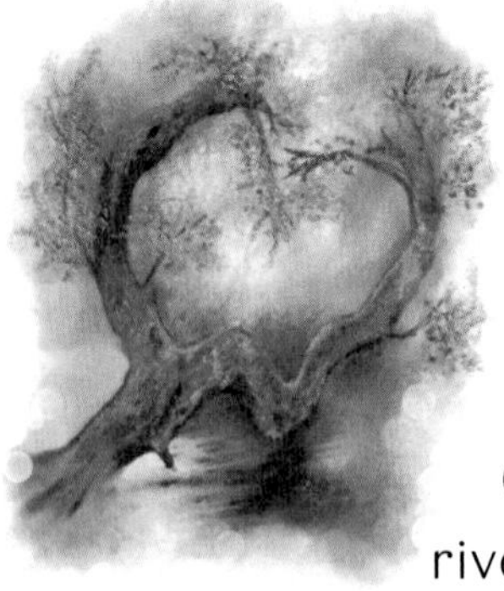

Opposite banks of the river are now connected by the fallen Love tree.

So the two caterpillars climb their guts
up onto the tree to cross the river
toward the delectable-looking flowers.

It's a risky venture, for they are exposing
themselves to hungry birds,
and maybe the tree will fall into the river.

By chance, the few flowers left on the
fallen tree find themselves
in the middle of the river below.
So the two caterpillars keep crawling
toward each other.

They are both enjoying moving
along the splendid Love tree.
And there is a gentle warm
breeze over the river too,
the storm having passed as quickly
and mysteriously as it had appeared.

For the caterpillars have missed moving
through the trees, without their leaves.
They've been obliged to crawl
on the ground for a while,
where they cannot see far and wide,
feeling free and in their style.

Strange as it seems, they both
head for the same gorgeous, tastiest-
looking flower that is drawing them in
magically, magnetically.

As they come upon it, they see one another.
They share a moment of surprise,
locking their eyes.

A curious unusual pause before eating.
They politely wait for the other to start,
a delicate gesture on both their parts.
And while they wait, they observe
admiringly each other's colorful capes.

Curious to take a closer look, they
spontaneously approach, and find
themselves side by side.
Then, as if by natural order, they
start to rub against each other,
starting with their guts,
to get a sense of who is this other.

Their caressing is progressing, meanwhile
they lose focus on the flower, lost in this
discovery dance, a Love shower.

Initially attracted by the beauty of the
flower, something else is happening
that's got more drawing power.

Beyond their superficial colorful veneer,
that maybe drew them curiously in
to peer, they find themselves in
a delir - i - ous state.

delir-i-ous

It's phenomenal, their shift of focus, for the daily life purpose of a caterpillar is simply to eat.

Their desire to have lunch has been turned to the other, because of a hunch.

Feeling they have something more in common than just being hungry caterpillars doing their thing, they remain in this open space, hovering over the passing river below, in a loving adventuresome place.

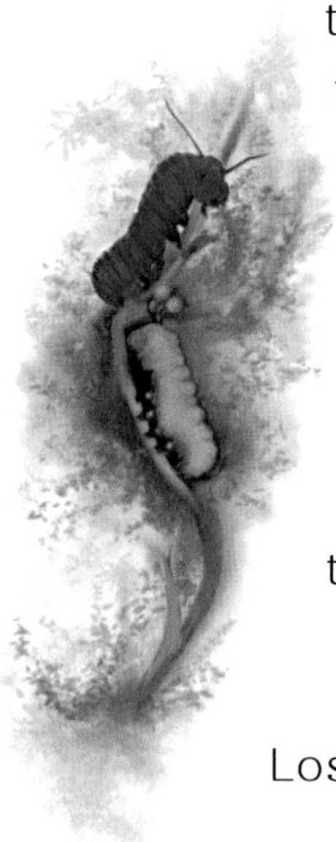

Exploring one another with their 4000 muscles, their wavelike movements dance together.

Lost in the ecstatic moment, they fear not even the hovering predator birds. They don't share any words. Caught in a trance, so very new, and happenstance.

To survive,
to thrive,
caterpillars put on a façade.
They decorate themselves.
, Like a veneer!
Some look like bird droppings!
Others so colorful they're
poisonous-looking.
Predators quickly lose interest in dead prey,
so caterpillars employ thanatosis
(playing dead), which often lets
them escape unharmed.

Their natural instincts to eat and
grow in safety have left them
for a moment as they play and
get lost in the other's feel.
It's a very deep desired appeal,
for each of them to experience
this intoxicating zeal.
Sensing this goes beyond
their superficial veneer,
That this is something so truly
and mutually dear.

Amidst the gentle warm fuzzy rubbing,
one of them proposes to eat.
Together.
"Come now, it will be so neat.
Love flowers make one feel
very complete."

"But first, may I make a toast?"
says Blue without boast.
"It's such joy to be with you here, on
this perilous Love tree.
Sharing this moment together
with such glee.
I feel so very, very free.
Golly gee!"

"That is such a delicate
beautiful intention.
You ARE a caterpillar
with invention," Pinky says.

"May I say a few more words?" she asks.
"My heart is aflutter, may I not stutter!"

And so she begins to share her heart,
right here from this gentle start.

"I don't know why
I've fantasized about being a butterfly.
As if I wanted to leave,
searching for some new
eternity to believe.
Some destination to conceive.

"When meeting you, I realized like so
few that the magic in this change
is something that will derange
who I am today.

"And to this moment, right now,
on this tree, with you in WOW!,
I realized I am all I need.
But have spent my life as a debutante.
Searching change in vain,
like a ghost on the haunt.

"And now I wonder,
in this heart blunder,
what is this thunder
arising in me?

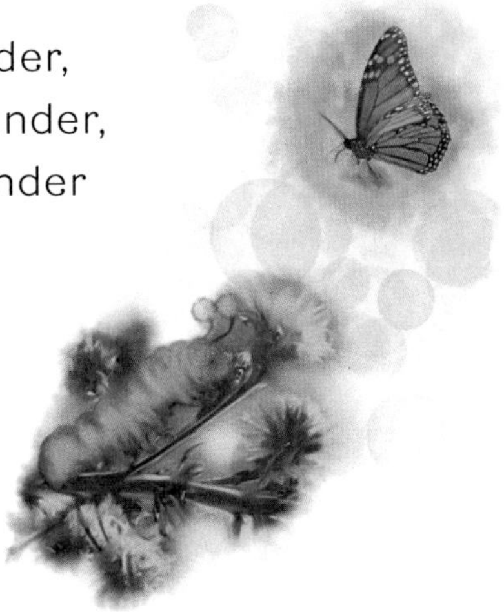

"Is it the way you make me feel, that
has me confused about what's real?
This feeling with you of my being
metamorphosized, something my
entire life's mission has prized.

"I am already now not the same.
This change thing, is a tricky game!

“I wouldn’t want to leave you here.
Unless somehow, my dear,
you have no fear.
And together we can pursue
our butterfly frontier.

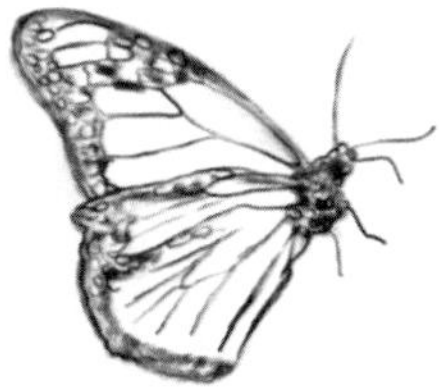

“All of this to say to you,
you have thrown my world askew.
Nothing will ever be the same.
And it’s hard for me to give it a name.

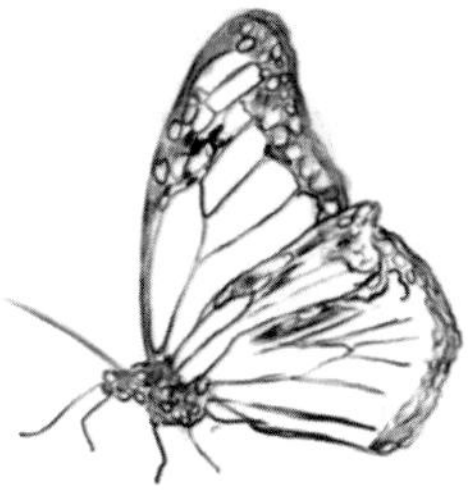

“I know in my heart, nothing is in vain.
That we both want to avoid
any useless pain.
Let’s hurry up and eat! Here
comes again the rain!
This all is really so insane.”

Blue is listening attentively to
Pinky, finding himself at a loss
for words in the moment.
So he instead initiates the meal, by
tearing off a Love flower to share.

Blue offers the first bite to his Pinky.
And meanwhile arises from
within him his prose.

"You are magnificent as you are.
We BOTH are a star!
While imagine if we could leap from
here, together, to a life over there.

"We just don't know where it'll take us,
which is why we are making such a fuss.
Is this butterfly thing really a plus?
Or are we falling prey to the
'do as the Joneses' trick bus?

"What if we tried to connect our
cocoons together by a thread?
Do you think we could pass
through to the other side
and then become
husband and bride?

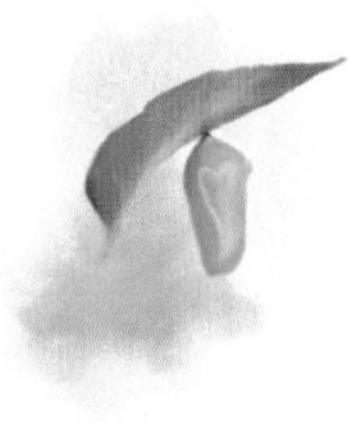

"Most of us caterpillars will spend
thirty days in the cocoon.
Some are faster and do it in seven.
And others stay more than a year!

"I wonder if we
really get this choice,
or does life choose for us?
And what if our timing
is all off?

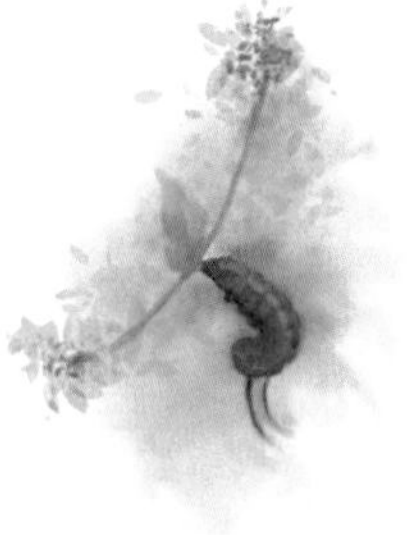

"We come out from the
mysterious cocoon ride,
and we're not together,
side by side?

"I've heard rumors that
we will change colors.
Your pink and my blue will
become black, orange and white.

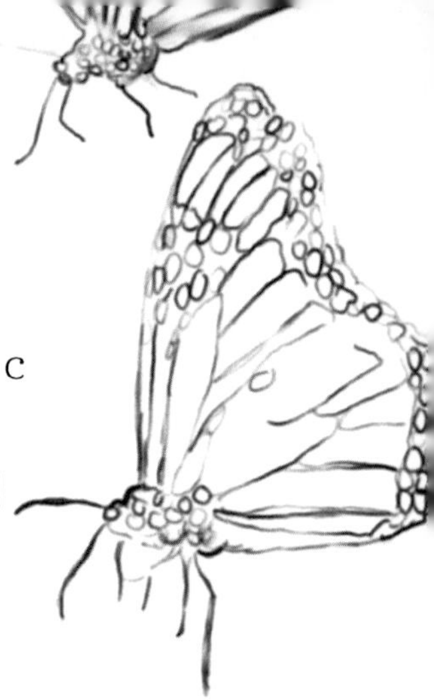

“We would become iconic
monarch butterflies.
One of the most reputed
pollinators of the land.

“During the summer breeding season,
other butterflies live for
only two to six weeks.
Except for us monarchs
who travel thousands
of miles to Mexico in the fall.

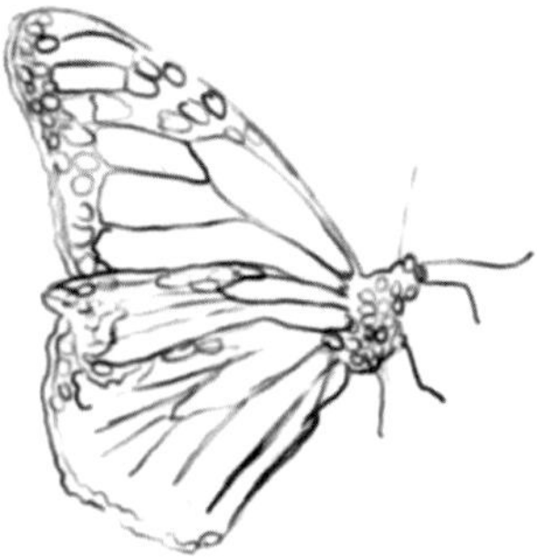

“Emerging in late summer,
we stay alive through winter,
then migrate north the following spring.

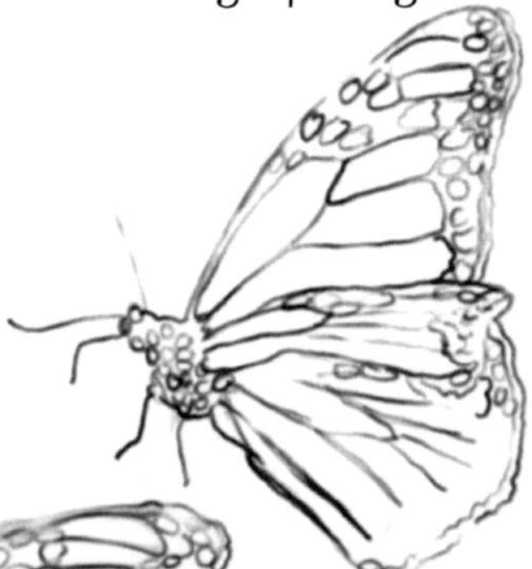

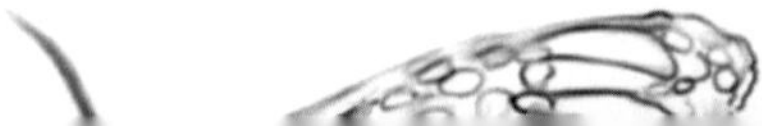

"This life as a caterpillar is so very short.
That life as a butterfly is pretty short too.

"And in the transition,
we will miss each other
from 25 days to seven weeks,
as we metamorphosize from egg to adult.
It's a very risky venture,
a true life adventure.
One in which all our ancestors
have been sure.
Is it only us who questions
this transformative destiny?

"For only ten percent of
us make it through.
That's little, it's so very few.
The dangers involved sound mostly true.

"We are vulnerable to weather extremes,
predators, parasites, and disease.
All this potential pain,
mostly 'cause we are
so low on the food chain.

"I wouldn't want to leave you
to become a butterfly,
knowing you are staying.
And I wouldn't want to stay,
knowing you'll metamorphosize.

"The clock is ticking for
us to make a choice.
Something around which
we would naturally rejoice!
While the consequences for us
together are mostly unknown today,
can we possibly imagine another way?

ticktock, ticktock

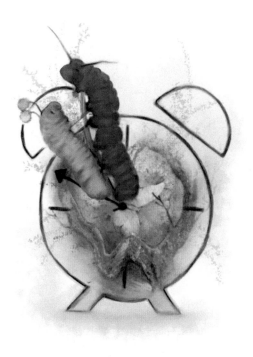

"From the instant I felt you, I knew,
and no one could tell me otherwise.
The sensation felt so true.
All that matters is our Love ties.
Not our form, color, shape, nor size.

"Nor even how much time
we have to be together.
To caress and appreciate
one another
like a Love feather.
And live together
no matter our life's weather.
Caterpillar or butterfly,
the question isn't whether...
we choose which one is better.

"Deciding we will share
what we can,
in the time at hand,
without some visionary butterfly plan.

"Although the metamorphoses
may be our path,
let's not waste a second
more on math.

"And savor this moment,
right here,
right now.

Together.

This shared Love bath."

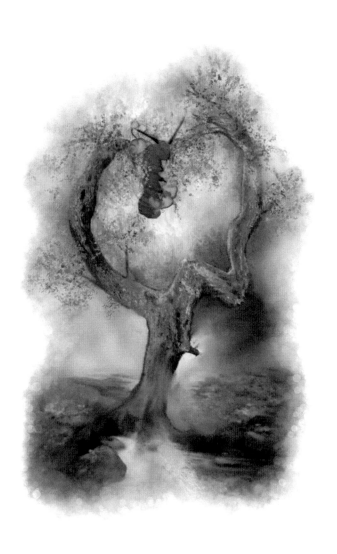

About David

David Brower spends his life searching for love and creating sensorial experiences everywhere he goes, wherever and whomever he finds himself with.

As the Sensorial Guy, and inspired by his own romantic personality, he inspires others globally to connect to each other in meaningful ways, to find joy in the everyday, create moments of romance daily and find pleasure in the small details and nuances of life.

Always from his intensively creative perspective, David expresses his love for life through writing, poetry, dancing, creating delicious meals in his professional home kitchen, hosting people, and helping others transform from the stage as a storyteller.

His lifelong work experience in international entertainment and cinema have shaped his love for the creative process and has been the catalyst for the creation of this inspiring story, *Dance of the Love Caterpillars*.

This storytelling gem is a universal romantic love story between two caterpillars, an inspiration to lovers and would-be romantics of all ages.

David, an American by birth, has chosen the city of love and pleasure, Paris, as his home for the last 30 years.

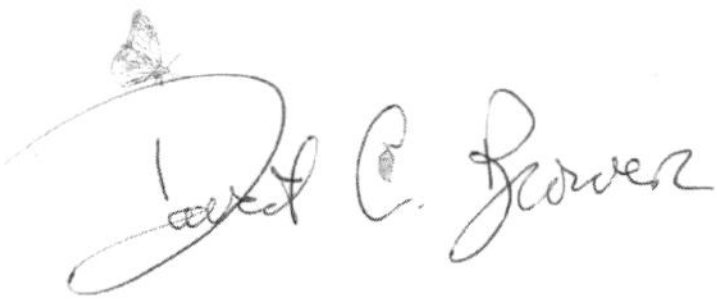

Now it's YOUR turn to start the adventure of loving, savoring and trusting life.

Connect with David Brower to explore creative and meaningful ways to live a life you love and love the one you lead.

Check his inspirational guidance and practices, and Sensorial Intelligence™ services, programs, writing, speaking and events at www.davidbrower.com

And meanwhile, always, savor life with pleasurable purpose, every day of your beautiful life, amidst it all.

Celebrate and toast your resilient abundant Alivefulness™, your way

P.S. Reviews for *Dance of the Love Caterpillars* are romantically appreciated.

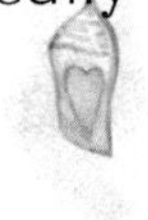

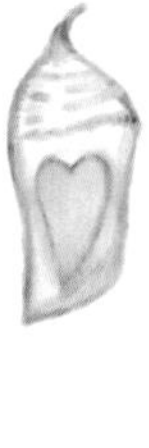

Made in the USA
Middletown, DE
02 February 2022

60288931R00024